REMARKABLE REPTILES

TURTLES AND TORTOISES

James E. Gerholdt

Published by Abdo & Daughters, 4940 Viking Drive, Suite 622, Edina, Minnesota 55435.

Library bound edition distributed by Rockbottom Books, Pentagon Tower, P.O. Box 36036, Minneapolis, Minnesota 55435.

Printed in the United States.

Cover Photo credit: Peter Arnold
Interior Photo credits: James E. Gerholdt
Barney Oldfield, pages 20, 21
Natural Selection, pages 6, 7, 15
Photo courtesy of Minnesota Zoo, page 11
Photo courtesy of Black Hills Reptile Garden, page 14

Edited By: Julie Berg

LIBRARY OF CONGRESS CATALOGING-IN-PUBLICATION DATA

Gerholdt, James E., 1943-
    Turtles and Tortoises / James E. Gerholdt.
        p.   cm.   --(Remarkable reptiles)
    Includes glossary and index.
    ISBN 1-56239-308-1
    1. Turtles--Juvenile literature.   2. Testudinidae--Juvenile literature.
    [1. Turtles.] I.Title. II. Series: Gerholdt, James E., 1943-
    Remarkable Reptiles.
    QL666.C5G47   1994
    597.9--dc20   94-10696
                                                                     CIP
                                                                     AC

CONTENTS

TURTLES AND TORTOISES

Turtles and tortoises are reptiles. Reptiles are ectothermic. This means they get their body temperature from the environment, either from lying in the sun on a log or in shallow water. Turtles usually have a low shell and live in the water, but not always. Tortoises usually have a high shell and live on land. There are about 250 species of turtles and tortoises. They have existed longer than all other reptiles, more than 200 million years.

This Red-footed tortoise from South America has a high domed shell, and lives on land.

*This Red-eared slider from Texas has a
low shell and lives in the water.*

SIZES

Some turtles are giants. The leatherback sea turtle can have a shell eight feet long and weigh over 1,500 pounds. The biggest freshwater turtle comes from the United States. The alligator snapping turtle has been recorded at over 300 pounds. Other species are tiny. The endangered bog turtle from the eastern United States is only 3 to 4 1/2 inches long. But most species are at least five inches long. The largest tortoise is the Aldabra, with a shell over four feet long and a weight of 550 pounds.

This is a Leatherback turtle. It is one of the biggest turtles in the world.

The Alligator snapping turtle has very powerful jaws.

SHAPES

Turtles and tortoises all have shells. The top of the shell is called a carapace, and the bottom is called a plastron. Turtles usually have low, flat shells to help them swim faster. Since tortoises don't swim, they usually have high domed shells. But there are a few exceptions. The box turtles from the United States and Asia have high shells, and the pancake tortoise from Africa has a low shell.

The plastron (bottom) of this Wood turtle from Wisconsin is very colorful.

*This Three-toed box turtle from Oklahoma
has a domed carapace (top shell).*

COLORS

Most turtles and tortoises have colors that help them blend in with their surroundings. This is called camouflage. But some, like the red-footed tortoise from South America, have very bright colors. A turtle with very bright colors is the Painted turtle from the United States. Male and female turtles and tortoises of each species are the same color. But most male box turtles have bright red eyes!

The plastron (bottom) of this Western painted turtle from Minnesota is brightly colored.

This male Eastern box turtle has bright red eyes.

HABITAT

Turtles and tortoises live in many different types of habitats. While a turtle usually needs water to live, a tortoise is at home far away from the water. Lakes, ponds, and rivers are a good place to find turtles. Even streams high in the mountains can be home to some turtles. The big-headed turtle from China is one of these. Deserts are a good place to find tortoises. But some, like the red-footed tortoise, live in the rain forest.

This Texas tortoise lives in the desert.

The Red-footed tortoise lives in the rain forest.

SENSES

Turtles and tortoises have the same five senses as humans. All of them have very good eyesight. Sea turtles can actually see through the water, onto land. Their sense of smell is also very sharp, and helps them find food. Their hearing is not good, and they can only hear low notes. Their sense of touch, even through the hard shell, is good. Hisses and grunting are the only sounds turtles and tortoises make.

This Big-headed turtle from China is hissing.

This is a Sea turtle swimming underwater.

15

DEFENSE

The shell of a turtle or tortoise is an important defense against their enemies. A box turtle can close its shell tight. They have a hinge with which to do this. But not all species have hard shells. The softshell turtles rely on camouflage to hide. They can also bite! Many turtles escape into the water and hide when danger is near. Sometimes they dive into the water before you even see them. Only the splash tells you that a turtle was near. The pancake tortoise uses its low shell to hide in rock crevices. Box turtles sometimes hide under rocks.

This Alligator snapping turtle is ready to bite.

This Ornate box turtle has closed its shell.

FOOD

Turtles and tortoises eat just about everything. Some eat only fruits and vegetables. Other species eat fish or any animal they can catch. Some, like the Matamata, lie under the water and attract fish with two worm-like tentacles under their chin. Then, they actually suck the fish into their mouth. The alligator snapping turtle has a tongue that looks like a worm to attract its food. If a fish gets too close, it gets snapped! Box turtles and tortoises are attracted to red food items. Most water turtles are scavengers, feeding on any dead animal they find.

This Three-toed box turtle likes to eat apples.

This Three-toed box turtle is enjoying a tasty cricket.

BABIES

All turtle and tortoise babies hatch from eggs. The eggs are laid in nests in the ground. These nests are dug by the females, then covered up again. But some species lay their eggs under rotting vegetation. The eggs usually hatch after two months. Almost all species lay their eggs and then leave the nest. But the Burmese brown tortoise will guard her eggs for a few days after they are laid. Some, like the black-breasted leaf turtle, lay only a single egg. Others, like the sea turtles, may lay over 100 eggs several times in a single year.

This False map turtle from Minnesota has just hatched.

These two Spiny softshell turtles from Minnesota have just hatched.

GLOSSARY

Camouflage (CAM-o-flaj) - The ability to blend in with the surroundings.

Carapace (CAR-a-pace) - The top half of the shell.

Ectothermic (ek-to-THERM-ik) - Regulating body temperature from an outside heat source.

Endangered (en-DAIN-jerd) - At risk of extinction.

Environment (en-VI-ron-ment) - Surroundings an animal lives in.

Habitat (HAB-e-tat) - An area an animal lives in.

Plastron (PLAS-tron) - The bottom half of the shell.

Reptiles (REP-tiles) - Scaly-skinned animals with backbones.

Scavenger (SKAV-en-jer) - Feeding on dead plants and animals.

Species (SPES-es) - A kind or type.

Tentacle (TENT-a-kell) - A long flexible body part.

Vegetation (vej-e-TASH-un) - Plants found in an area.

Index

About the Author

Jim Gerholdt has been studying reptiles and amphibians for more than 40 years. He has presented lectures and displays throughout the state of Minnesota for 9 years. He is a founding member of the Minnesota Herpetological Society and is active in conservation issues involving reptiles and amphibians in India and Aruba, as well as Minnesota.

Photo by Tim Judy